THE SECRET WORLD OF
Snakes

THE SECRET WORLD OF

Snakes

Theresa Greenaway

www.raintreepublishers.co.uk
Visit our website to find out more information about **Raintree** books.

To order:
 Phone 44 (0) 1865 888112
 Send a fax to 44 (0) 1865 314091
 Visit the Raintree Bookshop at www.raintreepublishers.co.uk to browse our catalogue and order online.

First published in Great Britain by Raintree,
Halley Court, Jordan Hill, Oxford
OX2 8EJ, part of Harcourt Education.
Raintree is a registered trademark of Harcourt Education Ltd.

Produced for Raintree by Discovery Books
Editors: Helen Dwyer and Catherine Clarke
Series Consultant: Michael Chinery
Design: Ian Winton
Illustrations: Stuart Lafford
Production: Jonathan Smith

Originated by Dot Gradations Ltd
Printed and bound in China by South China Printing Company

ISBN 1 844 21590 3
07 06 05 04 03
10 9 8 7 6 5 4 3 2 1

British Library Cataloguing in Publication Data
Greenaway, Theresa
The Secret World of Snakes
597.9'6
A full catalogue record for this book is available from the British Library.

Acknowledgements
The publishers would like to thank the following for permission to reproduce photographs:
Bruce Coleman Collection pp. 14 (Carol Hughes), 16 (John Cancalosi), 18, 19, 21 (Gunter Ziesler), 22 (Joe McDonald), 25 bottom (John Visser), 27, 28, 31 (George McCarthy), 34 (Jane Burton), 37 (Michael Fogden), 41 bottom (Michael Freeman); Natural History Photographic Agency pp.10 (Haroldo Palo Jr.), 11 top & bottom (Daniel Heuclin), 12 (Image Quest 3-D), 17 top (Daniel Heuclin), 17 bottom (Karl Switak), 30 top (Hellio & Van Ingen), 30 bottom (E. Hanumantha Rao), 32 (Hellio & Van Ingen), 39 (Anthony Bannister), 43 (Daniel Heuclin); Oxford Scientific Films pp. 9 (Ted Levin), 15 left (Michael Fogden), 15 right (David B.Fleetham), 20 (John Mitchell), 25 top & 33 (Zig Leszczynski/Animals Animals), 35 (Avril Ramage), 36 (Zig Leszczynski/Animals Animals), 38 (Eyal Bartov), 41 top (M.Wendler/Okapia), 42 (Michael Fogden).
All background images © Steck-Vaughn Collection (Corbis Royalty Free, Getty Royalty Free, and StockBYTE).

Cover photograph reproduced with permission of the Natural History Photographic Agency (Daniel Heuclin)

Every effort has been made to contact copyright holders of any material reproduced in this book. Any omissions will be rectified in subsequent printings if notice is given to the publishers.

Any words appearing in the text in bold, **like this**, are explained in the Glossary.

Contents

Life without legs

A snake seems to have an unlikely shape for an animal that catches live **prey**. It has no legs, a narrow head and a very long body that becomes narrower towards its tail. Its thin, pointed teeth cannot cut flesh or chew. Nevertheless, snakes are widespread and successful **predators**. Well-developed **sense organs** help them to trace and track their prey. Backward-pointing teeth grip their catch, and wide-stretching jaws mean snakes can swallow their victims whole. Some snakes kill their prey by stopping them breathing, while others inject powerful **venom** with each bite.

 Most fully grown snakes are between 50 centimetres and 2 metres long.

 Thread snakes and worm snakes are the smallest. Some of these are just 11.5 centimetres long.

 The longest snake ever recorded was a reticulated python that reached nearly 10 metres. The longest anacondas are slightly shorter, at about 9 metres.

 Although shorter than reticulated pythons, anacondas are much heavier. A large anaconda can weigh over 150 kilograms.

 Thin vine snakes are about 2 metres long, but only about as thick as a little finger.

 The smaller kinds of snakes can live for about 12 years, but some of the larger kinds are known to live for 40 years or more.

eyes
No eyelids, but protected by a see-through scale called a brille.

fangs
Pointed teeth for catching prey, and in some species for injecting venom.

forked tongue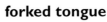
Flicks in and out constantly, picking up traces of **chemicals** from the air.

Snakes have been around for at least 90 million years. The earliest fossils (remains) found so far date from a time when their distant relatives the dinosaurs were alive. Today there are about 2500 different **species**, or kinds, of snakes. Most kinds live in the warmer parts of the world, although the European viper, also known as the adder, can survive in very cold places.

skin
Entire outer layer is shed when it becomes too small or is worn out.

scales
Overlapping scales protect the body. Large scales on the underneath help movement.

Just like other reptiles, the corn snake has a head, neck, body and tail, but where the neck ends and the tail begins is not easy to see.

SNAKES AND THEIR RELATIVES

Snakes, together with lizards, crocodiles and tortoises are all reptiles. Snakes are most closely related to lizards. It is easy to tell a legless snake from a four-legged lizard, although a few lizards such as slow-worms and blind lizards are also legless, or only have tiny back legs. The difference between legless lizards and snakes is that lizards have ear openings and eyelids, and snakes do not.

All of the organs inside a snake fit neatly, one behind the other. Ancient snakes had two working lungs, but in most modern snakes, only the right one works. The tiny left lung is useless.

Inside the long, narrow body of a snake, **organs** such as the liver, gut and kidneys are also long and narrow. Almost all snakes have only one working lung, instead of the two most animals have. Snakes usually have forked tongues and, like many other **vertebrate** animals, they have a **sense organ** in the roof of their mouth called the **Jacobson's organ** (see page 18).

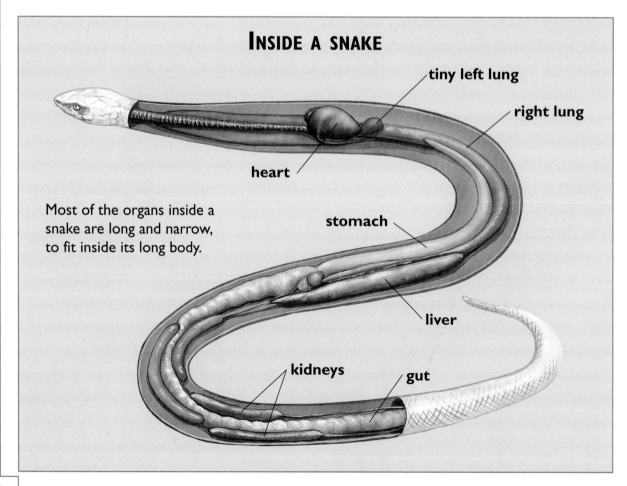

INSIDE A SNAKE

tiny left lung

right lung

heart

Most of the organs inside a snake are long and narrow, to fit inside its long body.

stomach

liver

kidneys

gut

Snakes and other reptiles are ectotherms, or cold-blooded, which means that they cannot make very much of their own body heat. Instead they have to live somewhere warm or lie in the sun to bring their temperature up to about 25–30 °Celsius. Snakes are most active when they are warm. However, they can easily overheat as well and may have to shelter from the midday sun.

Unlike **mammals** or birds that have a layer of fur or feathers to

In the USA, garter snakes return to the same site year after year to hibernate when the weather starts to get cold in autumn. Hundreds of garter snakes may hibernate together. They wriggle into holes under old tree trunks, or under rocks, and do not come out until it warms up again in the following spring.

hold in the heat, snakes soon become too cold in cool weather. Then they cannot move about or **digest** their food. Snakes that live in places that have cold winters, such as parts of northern Europe or North America, spend the coldest months in **hibernation**.

SNAKE SKIN

Some people think that snakes are cold and slimy, but this is completely wrong! Snakes are dry and often warm to touch. They are covered with overlapping scales. These scales are part of the outer layers of skin and are made of keratin, the same substance your fingernails and hair are made of.

Each kind of snake has scales of a certain colour or pattern that helps to **identify** it. Scales may be smooth and glossy, or dull, like like those of some rattlesnakes. The rough-scaled tree viper has scales that stick out so much that it is sometimes called the hairy, or shaggy, viper.

The scales covering a snake's belly and sides help it to move along. They also help to protect the snake from damage as it travels over rough surfaces. Because they cover

The gleaming scales of the Brazilian rainbow boa reflect all the colours of the rainbow as the sunlight shines on them from different positions.

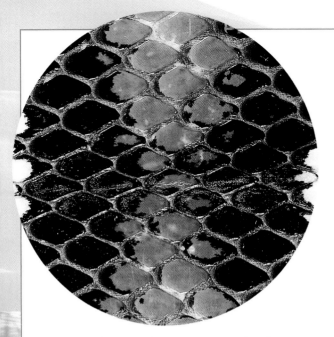

The shiny, smooth scales of a California mountain kingsnake are arranged in distinctive black, red and white bands.

A BAD NAME

Many people fear that snakes will do them harm. They believe that snakes will squeeze them to death or kill them with a poisonous bite. In fact, many of the most common snakes are neither **constrictors** nor poisonous. They are shy reptiles that are far more likely to slither away and hide than to attack you.

the snake with a watertight layer, scales stop water escaping from its body, so snakes can live in hot, dry places without drying out.

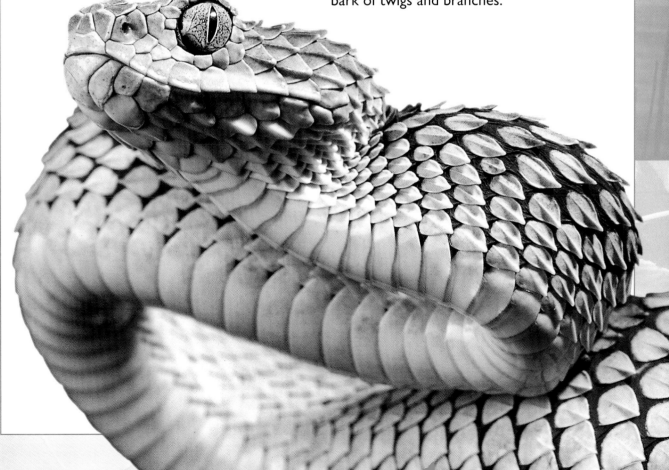

The scales of this bush viper are slightly raised so that it looks prickly. This helps the tree-living snake to get a good grip on the bark of twigs and branches.

On the move

Snakes have a very long, flexible backbone made up of 150 to 430 small bones called **vertebrae**. There is a pair of ribs for each vertebra, except those of the tail, and two pairs right behind the head. People only have about 13 pairs of ribs, but a large snake may have 300 or more pairs!

The backbone and hundreds of ribs support the muscles that make the snake move, and also make a cage that protects the **organs** inside.

 A rattlesnake moves at almost 3 kilometres (1.8 miles) per hour.

 A racer snake can reach speeds of 6.5 kilometres (4 miles) per hour.

 The fastest speed reached by a snake is 11.2 kilometres (7 miles) per hour, by an African black mamba.

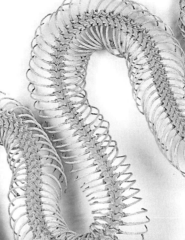

Only pythons, boa **constrictors** and a few other **species** have the remains of what were once back legs – two tiny claws on the underneath. Without legs, snakes can slither quickly across the ground, swim, bury themselves, climb trees and a few can even glide through the air. How do they do it?

 The flying tree snake of south-east Asia spreads its ribs and flattens its body so that it can glide from one tree to another – sometimes an incredible 50 metres.

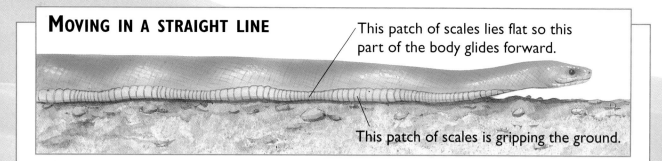

MOVING IN A STRAIGHT LINE

This patch of scales lies flat so this part of the body glides forward.

This patch of scales is gripping the ground.

MOVING ALONG

Along the underside of most kinds of snakes is a single row of large scales. These are attached to muscles. When the muscles relax, these scales lie flat. When the muscles tighten, they pull on the base of the scales so that the loose edges are raised. The raised scales can grip and dig into the ground. Patches of scales are raised or flattened along the body of the snake so it can move forward. Smaller scales along the side of the snake are also raised slightly to help the snake as it moves among plants or between rocks.

Large snakes travel over firm ground in a straight line. It looks like magic, but scientists have worked out how they do it. Travelling through grass or across a forest floor, small and medium-sized snakes wriggle through the undergrowth. The snake's head

The rough surface of the ground, together with tufts of grass and other plants, make it easy for a snake to wriggle forward.

When a patch of scales lies flat, that part of the body moves forward. When these scales are raised so that they dig into the ground, the scales behind flatten and move forward.

waves from side to side, and the rest of the body follows this path exactly. This kind of travelling is called serpentine movement. The snake feels everything around it with its raised scales and also by pressing the curves of its winding body against the plants and bumps in the ground.

SERPENTINE MOVEMENT

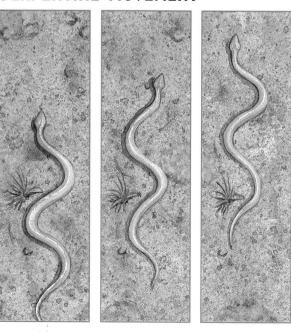

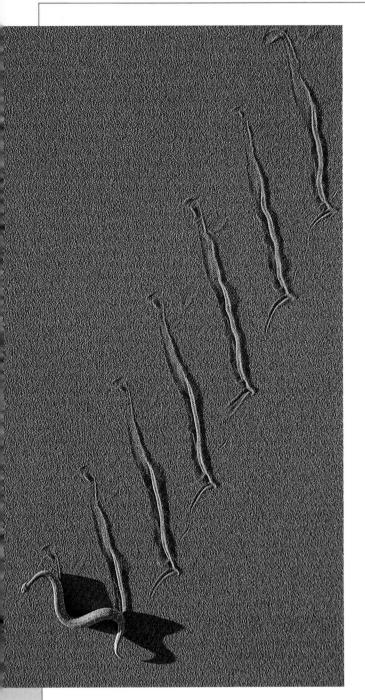

This dwarf sand adder is one of several kinds of snakes that cross the loose, dry sand of desert areas by 'sidewinding.'

flinging their head forward to make a curve with the front part of their body. The rest of the body follows on in these curves. The line of travel is forward, but the head is always facing sideways. Because it looks as though they are moving sideways, these snakes are often known as 'sidewinders'.

CLIMBING TREES

Tree-climbing snakes use the scales on their undersides to get a grip on rough bark or twigs. The coiled or folded lower part of the body grips on to the bark while the head and front part glide up the trunk. Then the snake grips with the front part, and the rear part of its body folds upwards. To make sure that they do not fall, tree snakes wrap their tails tightly around the branches so they can sleep or **strike** at **prey** in safety.

SIDEWINDERS

The sandy soil of the desert is too loose for a snake's scales to grip. The snakes that live in deserts travel across the loose sand by

This Arizona mountain kingsnake shows just how a snake can use rough bark to climb a steep tree trunk, even though it has no arms or legs with which to hold the trunk.

Swimming snakes

Most snakes can swim using a serpentine movement and happily do so to cross rivers. Grass snakes hunt for frogs and tadpoles in water, and anaconda snakes also lie in wait for their prey in shallow water. Sea snakes, like the one shown below, spend all their lives in water, where they catch and eat fish, squid and other sea creatures. Some, such as the yellow-bellied sea snake, also give birth in the sea.

Sea snakes are found in the warm coastal seas of **tropical** Asia, Australia and parts of the Pacific. Their tails are flattened in the shape of an oar, and act as fins to push the snakes through the water.

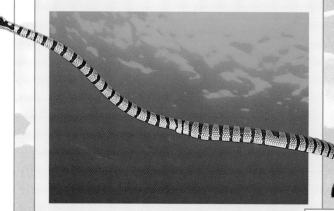

Snake senses

Snakes have to catch food, stay out of danger, and find **mates** and shelter. They have no eardrums and most have poor eyesight, so how do they manage to catch sharp-eyed **mammals** with good hearing and four legs that they can run fast on? A snake's **sense organs** help it to do just that. As well as using its senses of sight, hearing and touch, a snake is able to discover a lot of information about the world around it by tasting the air with its tongue. Many snakes can also pick up on very small changes in temperature.

Racers, whipsnakes and ribbon snakes hunt by day. They have large eyes with round pupils.

Nocturnal boas and pythons hunt at night. Their eyes have vertical pupils that look like slits.

Tree snakes need to see with both eyes to catch lizards in the treetops. They have eyes with horizontal pupils and narrow snouts, which mean they can see straight ahead and judge distances accurately.

EYES

Snakes have a staring gaze simply because, without eyelids, they cannot blink. To protect the eyes from scratches, they are covered by a see-through brille that is part of the skin. When the snake **moults**, old brilles are shed, along with the rest of the snake's skin.

Like most snakes that hunt during the day in bright sunlight, the parrot snake has round **pupils**.

A groove along each side of the narrow snout means that the long-nosed tree snake can see straight ahead as well as out to each side.

Snakes that hunt for food in daylight have the best eyesight. They are good at spotting movement but cannot focus on detail or **identify** anything that is not moving. At the other extreme, snakes that live underground have very poor sight. The tiny eyes of blind snakes and thread snakes are hidden by scales. They can only tell the difference between light and dark.

The bush viper rests among the leafy branches of a tree during the day. It hunts at night. Like most snakes that hunt at night, it has eyes with vertical pupils.

HEARING WITHOUT EARS

Snakes have no ears or eardrums. Inside their head, there is just one tiny ear bone that allows them to hear low sounds. Instead, with so much of their body in contact with the ground, snakes are very sensitive to **vibrations**. Because they pick up the vibrations from footsteps or pounding hooves they can move out of harm's way long before they are spotted by people or squashed by heavy cattle.

TASTING THE AIR

A snake has a long, forked tongue that it flicks in and out all the time. It can do this without opening its mouth because the tongue passes through a slit in the upper jaw. As it flicks, the tongue picks up tiny traces of **chemicals** in the air. It also touches the ground, picking up chemicals from there as well.

When the tongue is flicked in again, these chemicals are taken to openings in the top of the mouth that lead into a structure called the **Jacobson's organ**. This **identifies** the chemicals and sends signals to the brain. Different chemicals have different meanings to the snake. Some may come from a possible **mate**. Others mean food is close by.

▲ Like almost all snakes the copperhead snake has a forked tongue.

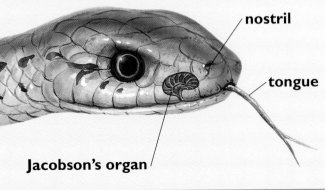

JACOBSON'S ORGAN
This diagram shows where the Jacobson's organ lies in the roof of the snake's mouth.

nostril

tongue

Jacobson's organ

SENSING HEAT

Birds and **mammals** are endotherms, or warm-blooded. This means that they can make their own body heat, so they do not have to lie in the sun to warm up. Many of the snakes, such as rattlesnakes, boas and pythons, that feed on warm-blooded **prey** have pits on their face or mouth that sense heat.

These pits are so sensitive that the snake notices changes in temperature of less than 0.001 °Celsius. This means that these snakes can not only tell in which direction its prey lies, but also how far away it is. They can **strike** their prey accurately in complete darkness.

Like rattlesnakes, the eyelash viper has a pit just in front of each eye that senses heat. If one pit picks up on a tiny amount more heat than the other pit, then the snake knows which way to turn towards its prey, even though it cannot see it.

A bite to eat

All snakes eat flesh or meat of some kind. There are no plant-eating snakes. Some kinds of snakes are not at all fussy about what they eat and will go for anything small enough for them to kill. The garter snake of North America is a good example. It will eat worms, insects, tadpoles, frogs, **salamanders** and even small **mammals** such as voles.

Some snakes eat only mammals. Others prefer insects, fish, frogs, lizards or even other snakes. A few snakes eat only one kind of **prey**. For example, the annulated sea

Snail-eating snakes from South America have long, narrow lower jaws so they can hook their teeth into the flesh of the snail and slowly draw it out of its shell.

The African snail-eating snake grips the snail's body, then hits it on the ground until the shell breaks.

The thread snake, which is almost blind, eats ants and termites. It may even live in the termites' nest!

▶ One of the reasons that there are lots of garter snakes living in many parts of the USA is because they will eat such a wide range of prey. This snake is swallowing a leopard frog.

Only the largest kinds of snakes, such as this rock python, can attack and swallow prey as large as a Thomson's gazelle. If it is disturbed while trying to eat it, the snake may **regurgitate** its meal so it can escape from possible danger.

snake eats only fish eggs. The largest snakes, such as anacondas and pythons, can eat remarkably large animals, including goats, caimans (animals related to alligators), leopards, deer and peccaries (animals related to pigs).

A GOOD CATCH

A snake only has its mouth and teeth to catch or pick up prey. Whipsnakes and sandsnakes are examples of active hunters that search for and then chase prey for short distances, but most snakes are happy to lie in wait for a suitable 'dinner' to get too close. From a coiled position, these snakes can lunge their heads forward at lightning speed. This lunge is called a **strike**.

Overcoming prey

After a successful **strike**, a snake has to overcome its **prey** quickly, before it is able to escape or cause injury with its teeth or claws. Anacondas and others of the python and boa family overcome their prey by not letting it breathe. These snakes are called **constrictors** because they squeeze (constrict) their prey by gripping it in their mouths and wrapping their bodies around it. Every time the prey breathes out, the snake tightens its grip a little so finally the victim can no longer breathe in

Once a boa constrictor has thrown its coils around an animal, there is no chance of escape. The snake's powerful muscles tighten slowly but steadily, until the trapped victim cannot breathe at all.

at all and it dies. Large constrictors have been known to kill and eat small adults and children in Africa and Asia.

Venomous snakes all overcome their prey with powerful **venom** that **paralyses** or kills the prey very quickly. Venom is injected by teeth called **fangs**. Back-fanged snakes, such as mangrove snakes and the boomslang, have grooved fangs towards the back of the jaw. The venom runs down the groove into the wound. These snakes have to work the prey to the back of the mouth in order to inject their venom.

Front-fanged snakes, such as the taipan and brown snake of Australia, have hollow, venom-injecting fangs in the upper jaw in the front of their mouth. After a **strike**, they hold on to their prey until the venom starts to work.

Pit vipers, such as rattlesnakes, copperheads and bushmasters, have the most complicated venom-injecting fangs. These long, narrow fangs fold back against the roof of the mouth when not in use. When the snake opens its mouth, sets of muscles tighten to swing these fangs forward into a stabbing position. A strike from these fangs results in deep stab wounds into the prey's flesh. Venom is squeezed from large **glands** by the tightening of other muscles, and it trickles down a passage inside the fang and out through a small opening – it takes just a few seconds. Then the snake releases its prey and waits for it to die.

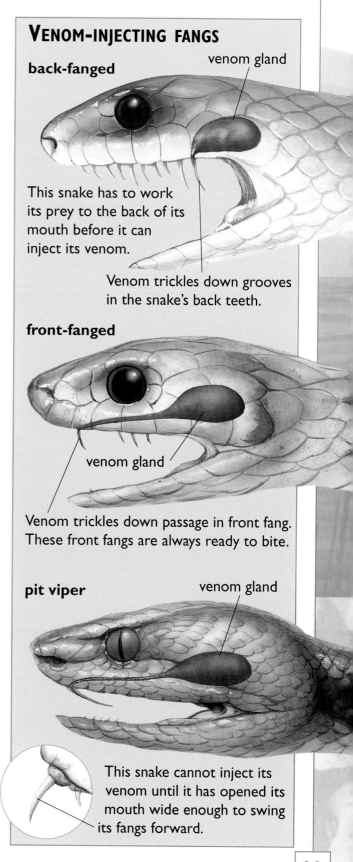

VENOM-INJECTING FANGS

back-fanged

venom gland

This snake has to work its prey to the back of its mouth before it can inject its venom.

Venom trickles down grooves in the snake's back teeth.

front-fanged

venom gland

Venom trickles down passage in front fang. These front fangs are always ready to bite.

pit viper

venom gland

This snake cannot inject its venom until it has opened its mouth wide enough to swing its fangs forward.

SWALLOWED WHOLE

Once overcome, the snake turns its **prey** around so it can swallow it head first. This way, arms and legs are less likely to get caught up in the snake's jaws. Snakes cannot bite off pieces of food, so all prey is swallowed whole.

A snake has to open its mouth really wide to take in an animal that may be even larger than its own head. So this can happen, the bones that make up the snake's skull are very loosely joined to each other. The lower jaw can completely 'unhinge' from the upper jaw. Each half of the lower jaw can move apart. The skin around the jaws is very stretchy, so it does not tear. Swallowing the prey takes a long time. The victim is worked back into the throat by movements of each half of the lower jaw in turn, helped by the backward-pointing teeth.

A large meal makes quite a bulge in the snake's body as it is squeezed down into its stomach. It also takes

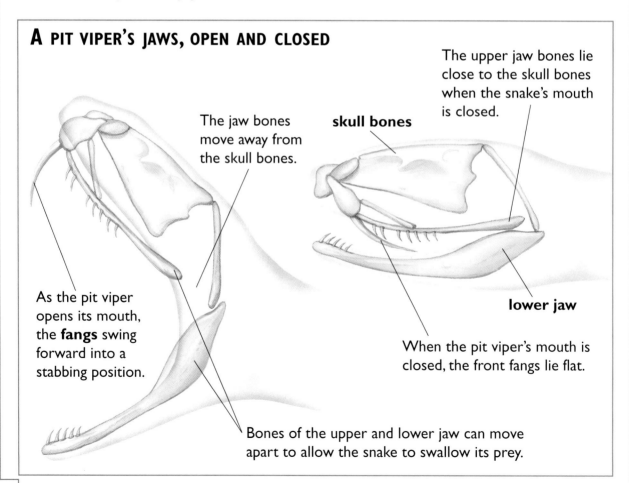

A PIT VIPER'S JAWS, OPEN AND CLOSED

The jaw bones move away from the skull bones.

The upper jaw bones lie close to the skull bones when the snake's mouth is closed.

skull bones

lower jaw

As the pit viper opens its mouth, the **fangs** swing forward into a stabbing position.

When the pit viper's mouth is closed, the front fangs lie flat.

Bones of the upper and lower jaw can move apart to allow the snake to swallow its prey.

Egg-eater

African egg-eating snakes stretch their mouths open wide to swallow entire eggs. As the egg is squeezed down the snake's throat, the shell is broken by sharp parts that stick out from the backbone. Only the **nutritious** contents pass into its stomach; after a while, the eggshell is spat out by the snake.

▲ As this timber rattlesnake swallows its prey, its throat stretches so much that the skin between the scales can be seen clearly.

a long time to **digest**, perhaps as long as several weeks if the meal has been a large one. After a big meal, a snake has no need to eat again for a long time. Anacondas or large pythons may not feed for up to a year after swallowing something the size of a deer or leopard.

Powerful venoms

Snake **venom** is really a kind of saliva (the liquid in the mouth that helps animals to eat). Some snake venoms are only mildly poisonous, but others are deadly mixtures of different **chemicals**, each of which affects the victim in a different way. The main purpose of these venoms is to kill the **prey** quickly to prevent it from escaping or hurting the snake. As well as **paralysing** or killing the prey, the venom also begins the process of **digestion**, which is important for an animal that cannot chew its food. Only about 10 per cent of snakes have venom strong enough to be dangerous to humans.

▶ As this copperhead snake starts to open its mouth, its **fangs** start to swing forward. When the jaw is fully opened, the needle-sharp fangs are ready to inject deadly venom.

 Between 30,000 and 40,000 people worldwide die every year as a result of snake bites.

 Although adders are venomous they are not usually dangerous to people. In the whole of the 20th century, only 9 people died from adder bites in the UK.

 The eastern and western diamondback rattlesnakes are the most dangerous venomous snakes in the USA. Their venom can kill a human adult in one hour.

 The saw-scaled viper is thought to have the most powerful venom. It is a small snake that causes many deaths among farmers in Africa, the Middle East and Central Asia.

 The largest venomous snake is the king cobra from Asia. It is about 4.8 metres long when fully grown.

 Vipers inject larger amounts of venom than cobras of the same size, but the venom of cobras is more poisonous.

 In 1991 an Australian man bitten on the hand by a brown snake died in just 35 minutes.

 The gaboon viper has the longest fangs of any snake. They are 5 centimetres long.

HOW VENOMS WORK

The **chemicals** contained in snake **venoms** affect the victim in several ways. One group of venoms affects the **nervous system**, causing heart and breathing failure. Another group destroys **red blood cells**. A third group destroys muscles. A fourth group also affects the blood, either by making it clot (stick together and form lumps) or by causing heavy bleeding. Viper venom generally contains more chemicals that act on blood.

Cobra venom mostly affects the nervous system of its victims.

THE MOST VENOMOUS

A bite from a snake with highly poisonous venom can kill an adult human in a very short time unless the correct **antidote** (medicine) is given. Snakes with venom

Although gaboon viper venom is not quite as poisonous as cobra venom, the amount of venom that the gaboon viper injects with each bite is much greater.

A well-**camouflaged** rattlesnake is hard to see. Often the first sign of its presence is the warning rattle. Ignoring this can result in a dangerous bite.

powerful enough to kill humans are found in all three groups of venomous snakes – front-fanged snakes, back-fanged snakes and pit vipers.

The most venomous snakes in the world are the front-fanged smooth-scaled snake and the eastern brown snake. The snakes that cause most deaths around the world include the Indian and Egyptian cobras, fer-de-lance, coral snakes, puff adders and some **species** of rattlesnakes. People are not the natural **prey** of snakes. Snakes prefer to avoid humans and usually flee from them if possible. They will bite in self-defence, however, especially if someone accidentally treads on or disturbs them! Anyone handling a venomous snake is also at risk – even snake experts are bitten from time to time. Female king cobras are one of a few kinds of snake that may be aggressive. They will chase anyone who comes too close to their nest.

A disturbed or threatened cobra rears up and spreads its neck. If its enemy does not move away, the snake lunges forward and may bite. The cobra family has extremely poisonous venom.

ANTIVENINS

If anyone is bitten by a venomous snake, it is important to know which kind of snake it was so that the correct **antidote** (medicine) can be given. Antidotes to snake bites are produced from the **venom** itself and are called **antivenins**. Venomous snakes are kept specially so that supplies of venom can be taken from them. The snake is 'milked' of its venom by pressing its upper jaw against the side of a glass container. This squeezes the venom **glands** so that the venom trickles down its **fangs** and into the glass.

▲ This snake is being 'milked' of its venom. This does not harm the snake, and the process can be repeated when the snake's venom glands are full again.

The king cobra needs its highly powerful venom to overcome the other snakes on which it feeds, but if people disturb it, they too will get a very dangerous bite.

Small but increasing doses of the collected venom are injected into an animal (usually a horse) over a period of about three months. The animal builds up **resistance** to the venom, and is not harmed. Blood **serum** is then taken from the animal. This serum can be used to fight the effects of venom on a human. It is called an antivenin.

The wounds caused by a snake's fangs are often no more than tiny

The European viper, or adder, is the only venomous snake living wild in the UK. Although the adder's venom is not very powerful, its bite can make some people very ill.

holes, but much damage can be done by the venom, even when antivenins are given. This damage takes a long time to heal because the venom damages muscles, nerves or blood in a wide area around the site of the bite. This often results in large scars.

Reproduction

For most of their lives snakes live alone, but male and female snakes need to pair up in order to reproduce (create young snakes). It is important that a female recognizes an approaching male as a possible **mate** and that she does not mistake him for **prey**.

When a female snake is ready to mate, she produces **chemicals** that act as messengers to any males in the area. Tiny amounts of these chemicals are picked up on the male's tongue and carried to the **Jacobson's organ** in his mouth. The male snake follows this chemical trail to find the female.

A group of snake eggs or young is called a clutch. The average clutch size is 3–16 eggs.

Some small tropical species may only lay 1–3 eggs, but these snakes may produce many such small clutches in a year.

The three largest pythons may sometimes produce up to 100 eggs in a single clutch!

These grass snakes are courting. The male wraps his body around the female snake. A fully grown female grass snake is bigger than her mate, as she has to guard and care for the clutch of eggs.

He makes contact with the female, eventually wrapping around her. If there are more males than females, then each female may be covered by males, all twisted together in a ball. After mating, males and females go their separate ways.

EGG-LAYING SNAKES

Most kinds of snakes, including thread snakes, pythons, ratsnakes and kingsnakes, lay oval or long, thin eggs with tough, leathery shells. Female egg-laying snakes often choose heaps of rotting plants in which to lay their eggs. As this rots, it creates heat, which makes a warm, damp place in which the growing snakes can develop inside the eggs. A few parent snakes coil around their eggs.

The Indian python coils around her clutch and twitches, which probably keeps the eggs warm.

As the young snake forms, moisture and oxygen (a gas needed by living things) are taken in through the egg shell. The egg grows, sometimes to double its original size. When it is ready to hatch, the tiny snake cuts holes in its shell with a special egg tooth at the tip of its upper jaw. It may rest with just its head poking out for a day or so. Then it wriggles free. The newly hatched snake may be seven times longer than its egg!

Snakes do not hurry to hatch. After breaking its shell and poking its head out, the tiny snake may rest until it feels strong enough to continue.

LIVE YOUNG

In the case of boas and snakes such as cobras, sea snakes, garter snakes, copperheads and vipers, the eggs stay inside the female until the young are fully developed. The shells of these eggs are very thin and soft. They split before the eggs are laid, so that the female gives birth to tiny snakes. The growing young of a very few snakes, such as the European viper, or adder, are not enclosed in even a thin egg shell. They develop inside the mother and are attached directly to her.

YOUNG SNAKES

Young snakes can look after themselves from hatching or birth.

The dull scales and cloudy eyes of this grass snake show that it is about to moult. After moulting, the colour of the scales is especially bright.

Many seem like smaller versions of their parents, but some have different patterns or colours that help them to hide away while they are still small and at risk from **predators**. The **venom** of even tiny young venomous snakes is every bit as powerful as that of the fully grown snake.

MOULTING

Although a snake's skin can stretch to allow large meals to pass along its body, snakes need to shed their old skin, or **moult**, as they grow. When a snake is about to moult, it stops feeding and hides somewhere safe.

The skin that has been shed is crumpled and inside out, but the scales can be clearly seen. A snake does not eat for a few days before moulting, so the freshly moulted snake may be very hungry.

Moulting starts when a milky liquid forms between the old layer of skin and the new layer beneath it. This makes the snake's eyes cloud over. After 2–3 days, the eyes clear. After a few more days, the snake rubs its snout against a rough surface until the old skin splits. It wriggles free, and the skin is shed in one piece. Younger, faster-growing snakes moult more often than older snakes.

Survival tactics

A snake has few of the usual weapons with which an animal defends itself. It lacks hard hooves or sharp claws, spines or horns, and is at a clear disadvantage when faced with a hungry, four-legged **predator**. Because of this, a snake generally prefers to avoid enemies rather than to do battle with them. If it is cornered by a predator, or

This red diamondback rattler is just one of at least 30 different kinds of rattlesnakes in the Americas. They are found from Canada in the north to Argentina in the south.

 The rattlesnake makes a warning rattling noise with the tip of its tail. If this noise is ignored, the rattler will strike, injecting its powerful venom.

 The rattles are made of loose, empty, pointed segments that rustle against each other when shaken.

 A new rattle segment is added every time the rattlesnake moults, but older ones may drop off, so there are never more than 9 or 10 rattles.

 When in danger, some snakes produce a large amount of very smelly droppings and then roll in them! This makes them less attractive to a predator.

If they cannot escape or scare away an attacker, all snakes, whether venomous or not, will bite anything that threatens them again and again.

Harmless regal ringneck snakes try to stay out of sight, **camouflaged** by their mud-brown colouring, but if one is threatened, it either coils its tail to show its bright red underside or flips right over, displaying a startling, bright orange belly.

has a nest of eggs to defend, a snake usually tries to scare away the enemy by threatening to attack. If all else fails, snakes bite to protect themselves, even those that are not venomous.

Scaring a predator off can be a good way to avoid ending up as the next meal. A common snake threat is hissing, which will scare many birds and **mammals** – including people. Boomslangs and hog-nosed snakes can puff up their throats when under threat, and puff adders inflate their whole bodies to make themselves look bigger.

A few **species** rely on sudden displays of colour, either by opening the jaws wide to reveal the pink mouth or, as in the case of the ringneck snake, raising and coiling the tail to show a red underside. This may not sound scary to you, but many birds are easily frightened by sudden flashes of unexpected colour.

CAMOUFLAGE

A snake's scaly skin is often coloured or patterned in a way that blends in with its background perfectly. Tree snakes are often green, with yellow or brown marks, just like leaves. Horned desert vipers are the same colour as the desert sand. Snakes such as bushmasters and gaboon vipers that live among plants or on a forest floor are heavily patterned to look just like dead leaves and twigs.

The Saharan desert viper, like other desert snakes, rocks backwards and forwards to hide itself in the sand.

WARNING STRIPES

Venomous snakes often avoid being attacked by **predators** because they are brightly coloured or patterned, and some harmless **species** also stay safe by mimicking (copying) them. Venomous coral snakes have a warning pattern of bright orange, black and white stripes.

Kingsnakes, which are found in the same places as coral snakes, look similar, but they are quite harmless. False coral snakes also look rather like coral snakes, but they only have mild **venom**.

PRETENDING TO BE DEAD

Grass snakes and hog-nosed snakes often pretend to be dead when they are threatened, in the hope that the predator, who may prefer live **prey**, will lose interest. The snake lies in an upside-down position and keeps perfectly still, with its mouth falling open – but this almost perfect trick is spoiled by the snake's habit of flipping itself upside down again if it is turned over!

Spitting cobras

As well as spreading their necks to make their heads look larger, spitting cobras have tubes of venom that open at the front of each **fang**. They can squirt a stream of fine droplets of venom straight into an attacker's eyes up to a distance of about 3 metres, causing blindness.

Enemies

Snakes have many enemies. **Predators** of many kinds feed on snakes, especially young snakes and smaller **species**. These predators include birds of **prey**, hedgehogs, wild dogs, cats, badgers and raccoons. There are also animals that specialize in eating snakes, such as snake eagles. Those that feed regularly on venomous snakes may not be harmed by the **venom**, or may rely on clever tactics to avoid being bitten. All snakes are in danger when they are young, but even when fully grown, many are still at risk.

Today, however, the most serious enemies of many kinds of snakes, big and small, are humans. Although most snakes are completely harmless to us, many people fear these almost as much as the venomous kinds or large **constrictors**. This fear leads to people killing snakes that actually help them by eating rats and mice. Some people just try to prove they are stronger or cleverer than snakes. Rattlesnake round-ups in the USA result in many being hunted, killed and displayed for sport. This is having a serious effect on rattlesnake populations.

 In the USA, large numbers of harmless snakes are killed every year because people mistake them for venomous copperhead snakes.

 The timber rattlesnake is no longer found in many parts of its natural range because people have killed and wiped them out from places near human settlements.

 There are about 19 species of snakes worldwide that are in danger of being wiped out.

 The New Mexico ridge-nose rattlesnake only lives in southern New Mexico, USA. It is at risk from habitat destruction and is now protected.

 Round Island boas occur nowhere else in the world except on this tiny island in the Indian Ocean. There is a serious danger that this species may die out.

Snake skin is made into boots, bags, belts, and trimmings for clothes, even though using some kinds of snake skin is against the law.

We are also destroying the **habitats** of snakes by cutting down **tropical** forests and draining wetlands. We are building towns and cities where snakes, as well as other wildlife, once lived. Many large snakes are still killed for their skin, which can be made into clothes, bags and shoes, or used in traditional medicines.

MONGOOSES

Mongooses eat a variety of insects, small **mammals**, and birds' eggs but are most famous for being able to kill and eat venomous snakes. These alert mammals are very quick on their feet and get tired far less quickly than a snake. They dodge the snake's repeated **strikes**, then kill it by biting the snake's neck just behind its head. A mongoose can successfully overcome a cobra over twice its length. Mongooses seem to be less affected by cobra **venom** than other mammals.

This mongoose has successfully caught and killed a large snake. It can now take its time and eat its fill.

SNAKE EAT SNAKE

A snake is a perfect shape for another snake to eat. Californian kingsnakes are **constrictors** with a varied diet that often includes other snakes, even highly venomous rattlesnakes. The king cobra is the world's largest venomous snake, and feeds almost entirely on other snakes. It is an active hunter and will even climb into bushes or up trees when it is chasing its **prey**.

This snake has almost swallowed another snake that must have been as large as itself!

SNAKE-EATING BIRDS

Many birds of prey catch and eat snakes. The secretary bird is a large bird of prey that lives in the African grasslands. It feeds on

snakes, lizards and small **mammals**. It kills its prey by stamping on it. Trying to bite the long, hard, scaly legs of the bird does not work. In the USA, fast-moving birds called roadrunners kill small snakes with a blow to the head before eating them. These birds move and turn very quickly to avoid dangerous bites.

In Asia, serpent eagles eat other small reptiles, frogs and small mammals as well as snakes, but the short-toed eagle of Europe and the brown snake eagle of Africa feed almost entirely on snakes. These eagles kill their prey by crushing it with very powerful talons (claws). The brown eagle can even overcome highly venomous snakes, such as boomslang, puff-adder and black mamba.

Even sea snakes are not always safe from birds of prey. The yellow-lipped sea snakes of south-east Asian seas come ashore in large numbers to lay their eggs under the rocks. As the newly hatched young wriggle towards the sea, they are an easy target for many birds, including the white-bellied sea eagle.

Snakes as pets

Having a snake for a pet might be appealing but is not always a good idea. Snakes are difficult to look after. They may need live prey, otherwise they may become sick and die. Some of the snakes that are easier to keep, such as the reticulated python, present another problem. Although only a few centimetres long when young, this cute pet might one day measure nearly 10 metres!

I DIDN'T KNOW THAT

Glossary

antidote medicine or substance that fights the effects of venom or poison

antivenin substance prepared from the blood of an animal that has been dosed with small amounts of venom. It contains specific antidotes to that venom.

camouflage colours or patterns that allow an animal to blend in with its background

chemical specific substance. Chemicals can be solids, liquids or gases in the air.

constrictor kind of snake that kills its prey by squeezing its body so it cannot breathe

digest turn food into a form the body can use to make it work

fang long, thin, pointed tooth

gland organ in an animal's body that produces specific substances, such as smells or oils

habitat type of place, or environment, that suits specific plants or animals

hibernation state of very deep sleep in which some animals pass the cold months of winter

identify recognize

Jacobson's organ structure in the roof of the mouth of snakes and some other kinds of animals that picks up particular kinds of smells

mammal animal that is warm-blooded and feeds its young on milk

mate (verb) joining together of a male and female to produce young (offspring)

mate (noun) one of a male and female pair that have joined together to produce young

moult shed the entire outer layer of skin

nervous system parts of an animal that pass messages around the body

nutritious describes food that helps an animal's body to work well

organ any important part of an animal's body

paralyse make an animal or part of the body powerless and unable to move

predator animal that catches and eats other animals

prey animal that is caught and eaten by another animal

pupil part of an animal's eye that lets the light through

red blood cells cells in the blood that carry oxygen around the body

regurgitate vomit or spit out already swallowed food

resistance standing up to or stopping something happening

salamander animal with a tail similar to a lizard, but with soft, wet skin like a frog or toad

sense organ structure, such as eyes or ears, that senses what is happening in the world around an animal and sends the information to its brain

serum watery liquid that can be taken from blood

species type of animal. All the members of a species have the same features and can produce offspring when they mate with each other.

strike fast, forward movement a snake makes with its head and upper part of its body in order to bite or catch its prey

tropical describes the hot regions near to the equator where plants grow all year round

venom poisonous liquid injected into the body of another animal by fangs, claws, or stings

vertebrae single bones in an animal's spine

vertebrate animal that has a backbone, or vertebrae, such as a snake, dog, or human

vibration quivering or trembling movement of the air or ground

Further information

Books

Animals of the Rainforest: Boa Constrictors, Sam Dollar (Raintree, 2003)

Classifying Living Things: Classifying Reptiles, Andrew Solway (Heinemann Library, 2003)

The Giant Book of Snakes and Slithery Creatures, Jim Pipe (Franklin Watts, 2000)

Keeping Unusual Pets: Snakes, Sonia Hernandes-Divers (Heinemann Library, 2002)

Usborne Discovery: Snakes (Internet-linked), J. Sheikh-Miller (Usborne Publishing Ltd, 2001)

Websites

www.hcontrst.force9.co.uk

www.bbc.co.uk/nature/wildfacts

www.enchantedlearning.com : search for 'snakes'

www.wildlifetrusts.org : search for 'snakes'

www.yahooligans.com : search for 'snakes'

Disclaimer
All the Internet addresses (URLs) given in this book were valid at the time of going to press. However, due to the dynamic nature of the Internet, some addresses may have changed, or sites may have ceased to exist since publication. While the author and publishers regret any inconvenience this may cause readers, no responsibility for any such changes can be accepted by either the author or the publishers.

Index

Titles in the Secret World of series include:

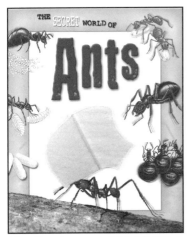

Hardback   1 844 21583 0

Hardback   1 844 21584 9

Hardback   1 844 21588 1

Hardback   1 844 21585 7

Hardback   1 844 21589 X

Hardback   1 844 21590 3

Hardback   1 844 21586 5

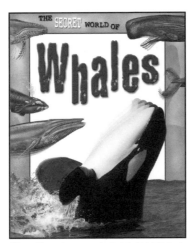

Hardback   1 844 21591 1

Find out about the other titles in this series on our website www.raintreepublishers.co.uk